RE-INVENT YOURSELF

BUSINESS, CAREER AND PERSONAL TRANSFORMATION

*7 Transforming Principles to Increase Happiness,
Work-Life Balance and the Self-Worth of Your Inner Child*

P A R A D E E   T H O M A S

CONTENTS

MORE RESOURCES

You can find more resources at www.paradeethomas.com

To my Mum and Dad, the rock and foundation of my faith and wealth, the source of my strength and character, the wind beneath God's wing that propels me to have the heart to embrace change; the boldness to step out of my comfort zone and the courage to reinvent myself.

ENDORSEMENTS

Paradee Thomas, an energetic and creative project manager, can turn her hand to any problem in any industry, the not so quiet achiever who has managed many difficult (and sometimes out-of control) projects back on track. She helps bring out the talent in people.

Observing how she applied the same philosophy to raising her children, I had the benefit of watching them grow from a young age to become incredibly balanced, talented and successful women. A credit to her parenting and her core values which she showed at work.

Tom Stianos, CEO and Board Director

Paradee Thomas has written a sincere and heartfelt book about the seven key transformational principles that are time tested to producing remarkable results for herself and her clients.

Her family stories provide personal insight on how these values created a life-time of success.

Lucy Hoger, CEO and Board Director

The principles outlined in this book really got me hooked! I have many favourite takeaways:

'Focus on what you want not on what you don't want. If you are stuck in the past the future will never satisfy you.'

'Are YOU EXCITED about your future or AFRAID of your past?'

'There is an aspect of security with behaviour we know and are familiar with even if it leads to undesirable outcomes.'

'There are no resistant listeners, only inflexible communicators.'

'You can't pursue your dreams if you are too tired each day…..find out what is sucking the energy from your future and subcontract it!. (my Personal favourite)

Natanya Full, Management and Business Consultant

This book is so beautifully written and crafted. It's simplicity is refreshing and inspiring but does not diminish the powerful and valuable message in the slightest.

The author illustrates many points using some of her own experiences that are so easily relatable and motivating.

I found myself pausing to reflect upon each of the 7 principles as I read them.

A very practical and motivating book. I highly recommend it.

Ellie Savoy
#1 International Best Selling Author and
Board Certified Holistic Health Coach

Books in this Series

Re-Invent Yourself

Business, Career and Personal Transformation

Book One
7 Transforming Principles to Increase Happiness, Work-Life Balance and the Self-Worth of Your Inner Child

Book Two
7 Steps to Self Transformation with Ease and Grace Reconnect with Your True Super Power

Book Three
The Secrets of Self Motivation Keep on Keeping on to Create a Life you Love; a Career you Excel in; a Rewarding Business

The best and most beautiful things in the world cannot be seen or even touched – they must be felt with the heart.
—Helen Keller

INTRODUCTION

Kites rise highest against the wind, not with it.
            —Winston Churchill

Why am I writing this book? My motivation for writing this book is to share what I have learnt over the past 25 years with men and women who have the desire to improve their lives. I have used the principles outlined in this book to reinvent my clients' business and projects, my personal life and my career many times over.

If this book can help one person with one idea that could help the person to transform his/her personal life, business or career then I have done my job. I look forward to hearing your success in applying the principles outlined in this book. You don't have to spend 25 years experimenting! You can leverage off the 25 years of my life learning, mastering and fine-tuning the principles of transformation that I dearly love to share with you.

I had a wonderful childhood.

Being number four of five children in my family allowed me to fly under my parents' radar most of the time. I made a point of getting out of everybody's way so I could do whatever I wanted! I had the freedom to choose to do whatever subjects I wanted to do at school. My parents never asked to see the school reports and I never made the point of telling them that I was the captain of my class and got top marks in most of the subjects! As far as my parents were concerned, the only criteria we – children had to meet was to study hard, go to university and get a good job!

It was an unspoken rule that my parents would take care of our financial needs and our responsibility as children was to study, study and study some more! It was a non-negotiable rule on our part. And heaven forbid, if any of us broke that rule, the consequences would have been unimaginable!

The hunger for knowledge kept me up very late at night doing homework. I loved to explore different ways of doing things in order to find the most efficient method. Simplicity seemed to be what I was striving for, but I was not aware of that at the time.

I did have a fair share of life with regular household quarrels and siblings' infighting like any other family! The way I coped with those stormy events was just to day dream away, pretending that I was somewhere else with a much nicer environment. I would imagine sitting on a beach in a far-away land where nothing can disturb my peace! I did not realise back then that I was practising the power of visualisation!

One of my favourite past times was to stare at the sky at night. When it was pitch black and clear sky, I would look at the stars shining up above and wonder: who is out there in that vast empty space? That empty space felt powerful and mighty! Can I draw strength from it? Would anyone mind?

What I Learned from My Parents

From my mother, I learned about having faith in God; the power of the universe and how that power can guide and protect me through the twist and turn of life journey. This belief had given me confidence in myself to sail through my teenage years and adulthood without any incidents I would later regret.

I believe what I learned from my mother was essential to my development as a young adult and later into mature adulthood. I learned responsibility and moderation, two things every life needs in order to see happiness and success.

From my father, I learned about money management and the distinction between good debts and bad debts. It was quite common for me to hear conversations at our dining table about investment strategies, some of which yielded handsomely and others not. It was not unusual to hear about interest rates and loan payments at the age of five. One uncle of mine even founded a Bank. Needless to say, his family was doing really well. This uncle was known to us as 'the rich uncle'!

I observed the importance of learning how to make money **and** be happy spiritually. So I grew up incredibly comfortable with both wealth and spirituality. I learnt at a very young age that money is a good servant but a bad master. Just like electricity, money can increase your quality of life or it can destroy you. It truly was a delight to experience even though I was not aware at the time that I was in an exceptionally blessed environment. I did feel though that I was an odd one out among my peers when we discussed the subjects of spirituality and wealth! As far as I was concerned the two go hand-in-hand, but I was unable to explain why. To most people, you would only be for one and against the other! Sadly, most 'spiritual' community lead us to believe that money is evil!

Realising this led me to wonder what the common ground between the two was. I wondered, *Is it possible to be spiritual and wealthy, and be a good person inside and out?*

This is a huge question for many people. Why? Most people are constantly told that money is evil and doesn't buy happiness. However, we all know that you need money in order to keep your house and to avoid the stress of pinching pennies; so money seems like a good thing to have. Simply having **enough** money can do wonders for people's happiness levels.

I wanted to understand the fine line between prosperity and spirituality. Can you have both and be successful? Following this interest of mine, I spent the last 25 years researching on the real meaning of *Success*. I have read countless books ranging from self-help, personal development, sales and marketing, to money-management. I attended every seminar and every course that came my way on the subject of *Success*. I read the Bible from cover to cover four times. The results of my research have given me an in-depth and priceless insight into a natural and powerful way of integrating the supernatural world with the physical abundant world in order to create the reality of life we want.

I was led to join a consulting firm in Melbourne, Australia. After over 25 years of consulting to large corporations in Australia and Asia, I found that I was able to help hundreds of corporate executives achieve their professional goals through meeting their company objectives, using the universal laws of success I learned from my mother and father, combined with the results from my 25 year research.

Special Talents

At school, when a new concept was introduced in class, I was often left dissatisfied by the answers given by my teachers when I would ask the teacher to explain certain aspects of the concept! I wasn't trying to be difficult. I just wanted to break the concept down into basic components that would assist my understanding. While I got good grade for the subject discussed, I was labelled a 'slow learner' as a result of asking too many questions! How would you feel about that kind of labels?

That must have dampened my self-esteem somewhat. Not that I knew much about the subconscious mind and how every little piece of information – good or bad- can influent your belief in yourself.

I remember as a teenager, I used to look at how people do things and wondered to myself why those adults did those things that way! It seemed unnecessarily too complicated to me and I often felt that those things could have been done simpler! But I dared not ask any questions in fear of being ridiculed and called a 'slow learner' again.

Have you ever experienced a similar situation where other people did not appreciate your talents and the comments they made left you wonder silently whether you were good enough or measured up to their expectations? Well, don't let them intimidate you! Be comfortable in your own skin.

I did not realise that being able to make complex things simple was a gift I had been given since young until I started consulting to my clients in business and project management!

I believe that **everyone** is born with their unique talents. They are like gifts from heaven to be used on earth! Do you know what yours are? Are you comfortable in your own skin doing what you love with the talents you have been given? Life flows much better when we love what we do and we do what we love.

"Everybody is a genius. But if you judge a fish by its ability to climb a tree, it will live its whole life believing that it is stupid."

Albert Einstein

For more resources, visit www.paradeethomas.com to discover your talents.

Doing what we love and loving what we do go hand-in-hand to recognize and fully own yourself, your future, and who you can become. Before we can get there though, I like to introduce you to principles that are at work, whether acknowledged or not.

UNIVERSAL PRINCIPLES
Flow Freely with the Universe

Have the courage to follow your heart and intuition. They somewhat know what you truly want to become. Everything else is secondary.
—**Steve Jobs**

I want to share with you some ideas that I've learned to live my life by. They're called "laws of the universe." They work for anyone, regardless of who you are or whether you're born into wealth.

These laws work continuously around us, 24/7. You don't have to be aware of them (although most of us are) or even believe in them.

I stress that you don't have to believe in them, because regardless of what you believe, these laws can either be working **for** you or **against** you.

You can get the most out of these laws once you're able to recognize them for what they are. They're limitless and can be used as often or as little as you like. There's also no boundary within which the laws operate. Can you imagine that? No limit and no boundary.

There is also no restriction on who can access these laws and apply them to their lives. That means no favour or bias. Money can't buy them—they're absolutely **free**. Doesn't this sound great?

So what's the catch?

Well, there isn't one, unless you count simply **using** these principles as a catch. Of course, to use something, you need to know how it works first, right?

Well then, that explains why some people don't use them. They either don't know they exist or they believe something completely inaccurate about them—as in they exist and work, but only for other people. I'll be covering that in more detail later.

As for the principles, these laws of the universe can't be touched, traded, or sold. We know they exist because they're **felt** through personal experience. That means that you'll **see** the effects of these principles in your life, much like you **see** the effects of the wind in the world around you.

Because of this, once you recognize these principles for what they truly are, you'll be able to trace their presence and let them work in your life.

I'm sure there are some of you who are following me completely with this topic. However, from experience, I know that there are usually more who still don't quite understand.

How can there be principles at work in our lives that we can't see, touch, or feel, and are completely free to use? Well, I already gave you one example when I mentioned the wind. People have for hundreds of years, used wind to benefit mankind and improve the quality of life.

Windmills were first built to help power tools that aided in milling grain for food. Today, these same wheels, although updated a bit for the modern age, help generate electricity, pump water, and the like.

See? Wind. It's all around us and **free** to use.

Another example of universal principles at your disposal is the laws of gravity. If you drop an object, it falls to the ground. The result is the same every time and we know that as a fact.

Well, maybe to you, the adult reading this book. But to a child, this principle has to be learned at an early age. To the infant, the law of gravity is not always so obvious.

Have you ever noticed the upset child when they let go of a toy or their favourite Sippy cup? With surprise, and sometimes anger, they watch their coveted object fall to the ground.

However, after several "episodes" of this, the child learns to keep what she wants and drop what she wants to see Mummy or Daddy pick up (for fun).

What about the laws of light and sound? Light travels faster than sound. We witness this every time there is a storm. First comes the lightning, and then comes the sound.

If you were to spot a tree in the distance, you might see birds. You can't hear them though, for by the time the sound wave from chirping birds has reached our eardrums, the pitch has dropped below human hearing range, becoming flattened over the distance. Until we can get closer, the birds will just appear song-less.

These are elementary examples. However, I often find them best understood when I use these examples that we witness every day, and yet we often think nothing more about them.

I've taken the time to explain them in detail, because it's the basis for which we're going to address the real reason why you're reading this book: Reinvent Yourself. First, however, we're going to discuss **why**.

Why and What

Wherever you are right now, you have dreams and goals you want to fulfil. You may have a career you want to change direction: a business you want to improve or a relationship you want to change. You may have a habit that no longer serves you anymore and you need to get rid of it.

We need to change with time. The world around us is in a constant state of change so how do we adjust ourselves to keep pace with it?

Young children are often asked what they want to be when they grow up. Then a few years later, the question changes to inquire where they see themselves in five or ten years.

I can ask you those questions right now, but I know your answer doesn't matter. In five years you can be a completely different person from whom you are today. But what good is that dream, if you don't know how to get there?

The next five years will come and go, and then another five, and suddenly, you'll be wondering where all your time has gone. Well, it has gone to: having a dream and wandering aimlessly without any **way** to get there.

This book is a roadmap that can help you get there. I know you have a desire to learn more, to achieve more, to go further. Don't limit yourself by settling for less.

This book and these seven principles will help you break free from the roadblock in your life.

Perhaps you've worked a job for years that you hate; or maybe you can just feel it in your bones that it's time for something different—a new career, a new skill—it doesn't matter. It's time! You need to get on the move.

Perhaps you've seen success but have reached an impasse. You're not going to stay at a place where you know your time has come and gone, so you want to break through and reach another plane, a different level.

Or perhaps you're the type of individual who still has your whole life ahead of you, but you have absolutely no idea where you should go first. Whoever you are, it doesn't matter. If you're serious about changing your circumstances and who you are today, then you've come to the right place.

It doesn't matter where you are in life, what you've done, who you've hurt, annoyed, or let down. **Anyone** can benefit **immensely** from these proven seven universal principles for success.

As it turns out, it's not just about hard work after all, but about what you know and what you do with what you know. Once I lay these principles out for you, you'll be on fire, ready to apply them to a personal or professional project, your career or business, even to raising your family.

Remember, I said there is **no limit, no boundary, no restriction, no favour or bias** to how often these principles can be applied and by whom.

I do have to tell you, though, as much as I would like to take credit for these amazing principles, I can't. I didn't invent them, but I did discover how consistently they work time and time again, once diligently applied.

And that's what I've done. I've applied them to my projects and even my personal life including raising children. Also, you should know that I'm not the only one who takes advantage of these principles. **Millions** of other curious minds who became tired of their lives got anxious enough to test them out—and guess what? **They worked.**

All you need to get started is the ability to **change** the way you've viewed the world. I'm talking about adopting a different perspective, and I know it's not as easy as it sounds.

For years you've lived your life by a certain set of rules, and it's all you've ever known. You know better than anyone if things ought to change. Chances are though, that if you're reading this book, you already know that what you've been doing hasn't worked, and I can tell you why.

It's possible to be looking at the same exact object but **see** two **completely** different things. Are they both right? Well, I guess that depends on how you **see** it. Take a look at the following vase.

There will **always** be one image that jumps out immediately to you. However, if you look a little longer, you'll begin to see another image emerge—two faces that are looking at each other. It's all about **perspective**.

For more resources, visit www.paradeethomas.com

KNOW YOUR AIM
You Must Have a Target

Efforts and courage are not enough without purpose and direction.

—JFK

Okay, so you're on board. You want this roadmap and you want it bad. You might be doing a good job at your work right now, but you know that perhaps there're some ways in which you can improve.

If this is what you're thinking, you're absolutely right! I'm not talking about the "constantly improving" mindset. I understand how tiring that can appear to some people. I'm talking about looking at yourself with an honest eye.

Are you happy? If not, find out why. This is your life and your time to be happy. That's where reinvention comes from. I want you to learn that there is **another** way to achieve **better** results.

Maybe you just want to be more effective at something, teaching or leading, for example. Perhaps you want to curb some bad habits, such as smoking, overeating, or a certain addition. What about your temper and using anger to get what you want? Are you abusive and intimidating to those closest to you?

These are certainly things you need to remove from your life. But how? Easy. Pick a target. Seeing the full picture is good and necessary at times for inspiration, but for practicality, you're going to need something smaller to aim toward.

14

It's not just about having a target, though, but it's also about being in the right **environment** with the right **mindset**. To achieve anything in life, you must have a target, otherwise, you'll have nothing to aim at and to set your sights on.

Without a target, you'll also have no way to determine whether or not you've hit your mark. Be clear and concise about your end goal. Get specific; also, be generous and give yourself no limits or boundaries.

What have you always been passionate about? What's your heart's desire? When you're working your job every day, is there something else you wish you were doing? What are you passionate about and gets you most excited?

These are the **talents** I mentioned earlier. It's asking yourself these kinds of question that can help keep you on track when it comes to determining your end goal.

I know these types of questions scare us. We don't want to appear idealistic. I understand that, but I also need to be clear and upfront with you about something. If you aim low, you're sure to hit your target.

If you're serious about changing your life, you'll need to clear the air of the "what-ifs" and fears of "appearing" a certain way to others. Leave all that behind and simply be honest with yourself. Being honest is necessary because it will help reveal a critical starting point that will affect these principles for better or worse.

Understand the Motivation

I need to take a moment to discuss motivation. This is important, because motivation is usually the starting point for every action we take in our life.

How we're motivated can tell us whether or not we'll be **happy** about the things we're doing, or later become depressed with regret.

If you've got a target or goal you want to see fulfilled in your life, that's great. But how do you feel about that target or goal? Are you happy, drawn to it, and completely ecstatic about the idea of finally being able to pursue your dreams?

Or do you feel a sense of relief at the fact that you're finally going to be able to get away? It doesn't matter from what, but you know that when you look around, you don't like where you are and you need an out.

Did you know that two people can be heading in the **same** direction but motivated by **different** things? I need to point this out to you because if you dive into this book looking for principles to change your life forever, but do so from a completely wrong starting point, in the end you won't find the satisfaction and happiness you were seeking.

I'm going to explain it another way. People are usually motivated to move **toward** what they want or **away** from what they don't like.

You can't drive forward in a car if your eyes are glued to your rear view mirror, focused on how much distance you've put behind you.

If you're looking to get away from the present or something in your past, then you're starting your journey wrong. You need to start by focusing on what you **want** rather than what you don't want to see true success. This point is critical to your success.

To do this, you must eliminate all emotions connected to anything else but what you want right here and now. If you find that you're swallowed by negative emotions from your past that you want to forget, you need to get free from those emotions.

This is absolutely **imperative,** because if you don't, anything new achieved toward your goal will be cancelled by those negative feelings. The good will never be "good enough" if you're stuck in the past; your future will never satisfy you.

Finding your motivation is easy. Ask yourself the following question:

Are you excited about your future, or
are you afraid of your past?

Your mindset is everything. If you listen to everything else and ignore this one thing, you'll find yourself in no better position than before, even if you do reach your goal. Wouldn't that be the definition of failure?

In order to reinvent yourself, you will need to prepare, train, and teach your mental muscle to adopt the right mindset. It needs to be fed and nourished with healthy foods to keep it from hungrily devouring anything it comes into contact with.

For more resources, visit www.paradeethomas.com

PRINCIPLE #1

Change the Way You Think

You can, you should, and if you're brave enough to start, you will.

—Stephen King

You've chosen this book because you want to change something about your current situation. In essence, you want to change your future. However, in order to change the path you're on, you need to first get off the path.

**To change our future,
we need to change the way we think.**

You arrived at your present position in life as a direct result of what you believe. You can't expect to reach another plane or level with the same thoughts that have caused your stalemate.

A lot of the pain that we are dealing with are really only THOUGHTS.

There are two concepts that go hand-in-hand with this principle:

1. **Say what we want, not what we don't want.**
2. **The mind cannot conceive the reverse of an idea.**

I'm convinced that many individuals have learned a type of backward way of communicating with the world. We start first with the negative, "I don't want this, I don't like this. . . . " and completely ignore the positive, which would be to state explicitly what we *do* want.

Imagine walking into a store. You're not quite sure what it is you want, but looking around, you find yourself saying out loud, "I don't want bread, I don't need milk . . ."

Can you imagine the growing frustration? The shopkeeper can't give you anything or even help you find what you **do** want. All he knows is a list of what you **don't** want and **don't** need.

Likewise, this world and universe cannot offer you what you want and need if you stay focused on what you don't want. This goes back to an earlier concept we visited when I stated that first you need a target.

Individuals wanting to bake a cake for the first time might not know the ingredients they need, but if they know what they want, they can find the information. I challenge you to take a day paying close attention to how you communicate with those around you, especially when you're attempting to verbalize a need.

Are you telling others what you want and need? Or do you begin telling people what you don't want and don't need?

The Reverse Idea

The second concept deals with training your mind to think positively instead of negatively. For this example, I want you to **not** think of a pink elephant or red roses on a bright green thorny bush.

Did you do it? I doubt it! If someone tells you **not** to think of something, you'll end up thinking about it before they're even done saying the words. Why is that?

Plain and simple, the mind cannot tell the difference between real and imaginary. That means that you train yourself not by thinking of what you **don't** want or who you **don't** want to be, but by focusing on what you **do** want and who you **do** want to be.

This concept is seen best with young children, and I used it with mine while toilet training them. Each night as a part of our bedtime routine, I would "play a game" with my children.

We'd touch one side of the sheets on the bed and talk about how dry they were. I'd say to them out loud, "The sheets are so beautifully dry, aren't they? Let's keep them dry all night. Dry, dry, dry . . . "

I **never** said the word "wet". I wanted them to focus only on keeping those sheets dry, and it worked like a charm. I don't remember my children ever wetting their beds!

The Conscious and Unconscious minds

I love how simple these principles are to explain. They're even easier to put into practice, although you might feel a little weird at first. It's okay though.

Do you remember how awkward driving for the first time was? I know for drivers learning to drive a manual, or stick shift, that at first the gears are definitely not easy to coordinate. What about remembering to use your mirrors to see around you?

After a while, though, driving became less of a mental workout. It's also a bit like learning the roads in a new town. The new stores and landmarks are awkward and foreign, until one day you realize that you drove to work without even thinking about where to turn, or even remembering what you drove past along the way.

This is what the unconscious mind allows us to do—respond and react without even thinking. This can be useful, if we're already behaving and thinking in a way in which we're pleased and content with. However, if we're not satisfied with our natural defaults, we can run into a bit of a problem.

I'm hoping that most of my readers are old enough to realize that what determines your actions has nothing to do with your will. In other words, it doesn't matter how badly you really don't want to do something—if your unconscious mind has been trained to do it, you will. It's that simple.

Our behaviours are governed by our unconscious minds. That means we need to feed this mind with the input necessary to replace our old habits that will drive the action which will result in the outcome we want.

At first, this can seem like a large task. After all, if you are old enough to realize that you react out of your unconscious mind, then you would have likely spent 20 years or more practicing behaviours that negate the future you want.

This is why Reinventing Yourself appears like such a daunting task for some. This is the part of the program that will take **diligence** and **continual** practice until it becomes a habit. Once you get this right, the rest will naturally follow.

Case Study

Not long ago, I was asked to consult to an electricity supplier to 'find' some $25M 'missing' revenue. At my first meeting with the Director of Operations, I was told that the company had spent the two years prior upgrading their computer system and had already looked into their account receivables in great depth where they were 100% sure that the revenue leakage of $25m was not due to bad debts or poor computer system.

I spent the next few days observing what was going on with the way the operations teams of around 200 people process their work. Knowing this Principle #1 too well, I immediately worked out a program to change the way the team members 'think'. I knew that unless I could change the way they think about their work and the processes involved, there would be no change and no improvement.

The following few weeks, I worked with the teams to adjust their work practices to the point where the 'work-in-progress' was reduced from $25m down to $500,000 within 6 weeks of me turning up! I can't claim all the credit. All I did was changing the way they were thinking and the success just followed!

For more resources, visit www.paradeethomas.com

PRINCIPLE #2

Believe in Yourself

You become what you believe.

—Oprah Winfrey

Say yes to yourself and give yourself permission to step out in faith to follow your passion and be the person you want to be.

Believing in yourself starts with **first being the person you want to be in your mind.**

Remember that you act out what is in your mind. You can't focus on being a more loving and understanding parent if you're focused on how little patience you have with your kids or how much they frustrate you. Focus on the new you, not on the past. What you focus on expands and what you resist persists!

Fake It

As humans, I've concluded that we are naturally critical and many of us are negatively bent. Be that as it may, these qualities can be changed. Think about how easy it is for you to do something when you **feel** like it.

Our **feelings** quite easily govern our actions. When we're happy, we smile. When athletes win a game or beat a record they feel powerful and exuberant. What do they do? They smile too, but they also thrust their hands and arms high in the air.

These actions are dictated by **feelings**. This leads me to another note, is it possible to **fake** these feelings you want to emulate? Some people would emphatically state "no," but Amy Cuddy says otherwise.

An American psychologist employed with Harvard Business School as an associate professor of business administration in the Negotiation, Organizations, and Markets Unit, Amy Cuddy is best known for her research on emotions, nonverbal behaviour, power, and social stimuli effects on human hormone levels.

In 2012 she gave a TED Talk delivered at TED Global in Edinburgh, Scotland. It has since been viewed more than 19 million times and ranked as one of the top two most-viewed TED Talks.

What did she speak about? **Faking it until you make it.** Her research **proved** that if we practice certain behaviours, we can trick our minds into believing something, **feeling** something we wouldn't usually feel.

She included in her incredible talk her own story, which was just as inspiring. She presented herself as **proof** that you can fake it until it becomes real.

So smile when you're sad and laugh when you're angry. If you're feeling weak, throw your hands in the air and keep them there until you feel powerful again.

Our **feelings** are so fleeting there is no reason why you should let them dictate your future. But when we focus on the negative feelings and completely ignore the positive, this is exactly what we do.

We act out what we think and what's on our mind. Our mind governs our body. There is a reverse, though. Our mind is used to our body reacting out of itself; but the mind can also **react** to the body.

Remake Your Mind

It is so important to realize that your mind needs to be rewired before you can move on. I mentioned previously that adopting this new behaviour and thought process would seem weird, perhaps even a bit crazy.

I want to discuss this concept a bit more. So far, I've been heavily focusing on our thoughts and, essentially, our beliefs.

For people who are constantly negative, they find it hard to be positive because all they've ever known was criticism. Where do these thoughts and habits come from? I can tell you right now that we're not quite born with them.

There has come to my attention a nearly universal understanding that by the time children turn seven, they have **completely** developed their worldview, or beliefs, about reality. This elementary beginning about life forms our beliefs about life in general.

Children arrive at their worldview through observation, whether good or bad, moral or ethical. They adopt the patterns they see their parents or other adults using as the model for their own lives.

It feels right. Never mind if it causes them pain or puts them on another road that's less than desirable. It's all they've ever known, and so there's an aspect of security that comes with it.

I want to enlighten you to the fact, or possibility, that perhaps there's a better way to live your life—a way that will bring you much more joy and satisfaction.

The catch is that you must step out of your comfort zone and into the unknown. You must be willing to adopt new methods of handling familiar situations. Also, you must drop your old excuses that have "worked" for so long.

The past belongs in the past; but, the future is yours. Forget about what you didn't have or always wanted. Too often we're afraid that if we change, we're admitting that something didn't work—we failed.

Again, it's all how **you** decide to view your life. If I started from nothing and tried 27 different times until I found the way that works, I'd be happy and satisfied. Staying worried about how changing your approach to life will **look** to others will only keep you from pursuing your own happiness. So what's it going to be?

When I turn up to many of my clients' engagements involving projects that have been delayed for one reason or another, it is very common to find that the team members have already been burned out, tired and lost the belief in themselves! They have already tried many times to hit the project target dates with no avail.

In order to 'reinvent' the project team to the point where they could kick goals again, each member needs to believe in him/herself or there would be no change to the project as a whole.

For more resources, visit www.paradeethomas.com

PRINCIPLE #3

Tune into the Right Station

Failure is the condiment that gives success its flavour.
—Truman Capote

Changing isn't easy. If you grow up listening to one particular type of music, your ears will be more accustomed to it than to any other type of music. In fact, you might even find that you **prefer** the music from your youth to any other music that you might be introduced to later.

There's no reason for this, other than it is most familiar to you. However, if you want to change what you hear, you'll need to change the frequency you're tuned to.

Start by turning off the station that's putting out the messages and beliefs that do not serve you anymore. You get what you pay attention to, and if you focus on the right messages and beliefs, you'll be much more likely to achieve a better life results than otherwise.

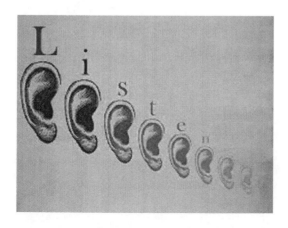

I want you to think about this deeply before we move on. I'm talking about settling. It's what humans naturally do. Perhaps we're too tired to hold out, or we don't know where to look—I'm not entirely sure what entices us to give up our happiness for something less than what we want.

What I do know is that it happens more often than not, and at the end of our lives, many people have either come to embrace the world they created, or they regret it.

If you want the ability to think outside the box and 'recreate' your mind, you'll need to **surround** yourself with others who think the same way. Model yourself after someone who has already achieved the results you want. Tune into what he/she is thinking.

The best way to do this is to find a mentor who can lift you higher and faster, because they've already forged the path you want. A mentor will test and challenge your thoughts and comfort zone, teaching you how to let go of preconceived ideas, to stretch your mind further than what you could do on your own.

> *Once stretched to new heights, the mind never returns to its original condition.*
> **—Albert Einstein**

We attract in our lives what we give attention to. I'm talking about the **law of attraction** now. Are you familiar with the Reticular Activating System (RAS)?

It's an information-filtering system used in our brains. It's most referenced as the function of our brains that dampens the effects of repeated stimuli, such as loud noises. It keeps your senses from being overloaded.

This explains why after moving into a new neighbourhood, the night time train is sometimes exciting and new, but after a time it no longer registers in your mind. Or what about the crowing roosters in the wee hours of the morning on a hillside farm?

It's also the reason why mothers hear their babies during the night and why soldiers in combat zones become tolerant and complacent to distant gunfire.

When something is a priority to you, your brain's RAS will **deafen** other stimuli to **ensure** that you won't miss what's important. Help it out by giving yourself quiet time each day. No TV or music. Learn to embrace silence so you can actually hear yourself think.

We are both a **sending and receiving station.** You receive stimuli all day long, but if you're not focused on it, your RAS will deafen the sound, and focus on past priorities and goals.

A good mentor can help you rewire your RAS to pick up the new stimuli that you want to receive. Being in a Mastermind and rubbing shoulders with like-minded people can help stretch your imagination to see the possibilities that you would never be able to see on your own.

Protect your mind from harmful negativity and criticism which are **everywhere,** especially if you're looking to forge your own path and do things your own way. The only way you can keep the bad out and keep the good coming in is to change the way your mind filters the messages it receives.

For more resources, visit www.paradeethomas.com

PRINCIPLE #4
Ask Better Questions

Do not pray for an easy life, pray for the strength to endure a difficult one.

—Bruce Lee

Learning **effective** communication is a huge part of Reinventing Yourself. Think about how much time you spend trying to undo a message you communicated wrongly the first time.

It gets frustrating after a while and can become extremely discouraging. Communicating is the only way we tell others what we **want** and **need**. Shouldn't this be something we devote a significant amount of energy to?

Foreigners experience frustration most in communication when going overseas for the first time. They have to ask for directions, often with intense hand movement and arm-waving, sometimes with no avail!

Naturally, they communicate in ways they're most comfortable with, only to find that to get what they want, they have to find new ways of talking and expressing. I do not believe that there are resistant listeners in the world, only inflexible communicators.

You might have heard of Columbo, a famous detective (much like Sherlock Holmes), who is a brilliant 'simple detective' who asks all the right questions again and again until he solves the murder mystery.

In my own life, I've learned a lot about communication from raising my children. Early on I realized that I needed to change how I asked questions if I wanted clearer answers.

One day before leaving for school I asked my children, "Have you got your lunch?" My children replied with a hearty, "Yes!" However, after work I learned that their lunches were still on the kitchen bench!

I realized that I didn't communicate my intent clearly. The next day, I asked, "Is your lunch in your bag?"

This is another concept that plays off an earlier principle. Do you recall which one? I'm referring to the first principle, where we discussed two important concepts about our minds:

1. **Say what we want, not what we don't want.**
2. **The mind cannot conceive the reverse of an idea.**

It's easy to fall into the trap of wanting those around us to instinctively understand what we **mean**. However, this type of thinking is rudimentary and immature at best.

Instead of taking ownership of **our** minds and our ability to communicate, when we think along these lines, we place **others** responsible for understanding **our** intentions! Perhaps this type of guilt "works" for some, but in my experience, people who **refuse** to adopt better methods of communication usually push others away.

In the previous example of my children, I could have angrily insisted that "they should have known" what I meant. I mean, wasn't it **obvious**? The truth is that if it were obvious, then they would have understood.

Remember, say what you **do** want, not what you **don't** want. Yes, this requires you to be quite in tune to what you really want, from your children, spouse, family members, co-workers, and other individuals you come into contact with on a regular basis. It means you can't simply open your mouth and speak and expect things to happen the first time.

Poor communication is perhaps an individual's greatest pitfall, and especially if it is continually neglected out of pride and arrogance. If you desire to communicate effectively, you must first understand **what** it is you wish to communicate.

Questions are the fuel for knowledge. Would Sir Isaac Newton have discovered gravity if he had not asked the critical question of **why** the apple fell?

As a consultant, every time I start a new project, there are many questions I need to ask my clients and team members to know what is going on in order to determine the right course of action! Most of us have been taught to ask open-ended questions with what, how, where and why, and to avoid close-ended questions.

In my years of experience in consulting to corporate clients, I have found that just using the technique of open-ended questioning is not sufficient to get down to solving the real core problems which are usually systemic and subconsciously accepted as 'normal' by the people involved. You might have been on one of these projects yourself in the past where you turned up to work every day knowing that the project (or the business) was not going anywhere fast and it was doomed to fail but no one had the courage to either make hard decisions to change it, accept help or call it a quit!

Three types of questions I ask.

There is no one particular type of questions I start first. I would start with any of these three types and rotate them appropriately according to the answers I receive from the previous question.

Ask Aspiring Questions I love this type of questions because it helps me rule out very quickly those negative team members! For example, I would ask 'Who else has done this successfully before?' 'What can we do to **model** from other successful projects?' Inevitably, those who have the desire to make it work would immediately step up to the mark and offer options to explore.

By asking aspiring questions, you will be able to weed out very quickly those people around you who are 'knockers', who say 'it can't be done', 'who do you think you are to try to make changes in your life, your career or your business?', 'you are too old to change', 'you are too young to start a business' etc. You want to search out and **model** from those who have blazed the trail before you. The best way to do this is to find a **mentor**.

Ask Exploratory Questions This type of questions blends nicely to a brainstorming environment where you can explore the different potential solutions and options. Look at the pros and cons of each options based on its own **potential outcomes**.

An ideal place to do this is in a mastermind group where the members have your interest at heart. They will have nothing to lose and nothing to gain. They will not sugar coat the message to you.

Ask Directional Questions this is where you start testing the water after having thought through options, consequential outcomes, your preferences and likelihood of success. You would then ask whether you should do 'THIS' or 'THAT', and 'WHY'.

The answer to a directional question will give you a starting point from which to proceed. The opposite effect is also true. I often use a question of this type, with ridiculous 'THIS' or 'THAT', to provoke ideas and discussions which I then direct the conversation towards a brain storming nature (the effect of an exploratory question). This trick is ideal to use in a situation where people may freak out if you tell them you want to have a brain storming with them!

You can use this in your day to day living. A couple used to agonise over where to go for a night out. Every time the husband would ask the wife where she wants to go for dinner, she would always say anywhere would do! One day the husband started to ask a directional question to trigger a decision or at least some discussion on the matter. He asked, 'would you like Japanese or Chinese tonight?'

For more resources, visit www.paradeethomas.com

PRINCIPLE #5
Keep Things Simple

All you need in this life is ignorance and confidence; then success is sure.

—Mark Twain

Life is by no means easy. With so many different ways to pursue the same goal, things can easily become cluttered. Our fifth principle is derived from the fact that **a confused mind will simply not take action.**

If you're looking to start something, it's critical to maintain clarity in your thinking. Unclutter your mind. This principle goes hand-in-hand with Principle #3, where I talked about tuning in to the right station.

Feed your mind **only** with what is necessary and essential to the current task. You will have to know how to say "no" and keep yourself from being consumed with overly complicated situations.

I like to think of the little clutters of life as dangerous distracters, because they take your focus off your true goal and make you sweat the small stuff.

Subsequently, they also take your energy. This is huge. You can't pursue your dreams if you're too tired each day. What's taking your energy? Is something keeping you up at night?

Find out what is sucking the energy from your future and subcontract it to be someone else's problem. This is how you rise above your circumstances and take a helicopter view of your life.

Pursuing your dreams is nice, but sometimes, the day-in and day-out routine can get a bit monotonous. You can lose sight of your future, take on too many dreary tasks, and completely lose sight of your goal.

Can you see why having a target is so important? If your eyes stay focused on the goal, you will learn how to immediately spot the tasks that will threaten to drain you of your energy. When you feel overwhelmed, go back to basics.

Don't forget what you're working toward. Keeping your life simple and maintaining the clarity of thinking will help preserve your strength and energy for the tasks that you must take on. I have witnessed time and time again on my clients' projects that wherever I see a complicated process, there lies a mind that lacks clarity of thinking! A complex process does not need to be complicated! A complex process can always be broken down to a series of clear and concise executable steps.

When one of my school teachers labelled me as a 'slow learner' despite my good marks for the subjects this teacher taught, I did not realise at the time that my dissatisfaction by her answers to my questions was because I detected the 'lack of clarity' in her explanation and I wanted to get to the core of the real answers!

Now I know that I have been given a gift of unpacking complex matters into simple components. This gift has served me well in my business and project management consulting career for over 25 years. What about you? Do you know your special gifts and talents? If breaking things down into simple executable steps is not your strength, don't struggle with it. Get help! Hire someone else to help you do it for you or with you. Spend your valuable time in areas that you are good at.

Visit www.paradeethomas.com for more resources to discover your talents.

Beautiful things in life can be made up of just a few simple components. Consider how a music composer writes many different and varying pieces of beautiful music from just a simple construct of seven notes, sharps and flats, and a few octaves.

Make your work light by breaking up large tasks into smaller sections and group like things together. Keep things as simple as possible. There are a lot of services available to help lighten the daily loads that our responsibilities carry. Check out online sites, such as Errund and Task Rabbit (primarily US oriented).

Hire someone to drop your clothes off or pick them up from the dry cleaners. Get a housekeeping service to help with the dishes, do the laundry, clean the house, or mow the lawn. Have you ever wondered why successful people don't take their own phone calls? They simply don't have the time.

If it's important, they choose to return the call later but at the moment, checking phone messages and emails is a huge time consumer. Subcontract what you can afford to in order to keep you focused on your target.

If you want to start thinking of yourself as a different and new successful professional, you'll have to start **viewing** yourself as one. Learning to let go of certain tasks can be hard for some individuals.

Perhaps you've always been the one to do it and you're not convinced that you'll like the way another person will complete the same task. These types of people often refuse help and complain **often** about their daily responsibilities.

This principle is so important because there does come a point when a person's tasks are simply too much. I knew a stay-at-home mother who eventually gave up on laundry. After complaining for months about not having enough time for her children throughout the day because of laundry, she finally realized that her time was more important. She and her husband budgeted for a laundry service and everyone in their home was happier.

Mum was no longer bogged down with endless loads of laundry to wash, fold, and put away. Dad no longer had to hear about all the laundry that needed to be done; and the young children were able to enjoy their parents more.

I mention this point because with certain jobs there often comes a type of ownership mentality that can keep us from keeping things simple. This is best seen with mothers, when they feel as if many household responsibilities are solely theirs alone. That includes laundry; meals for breakfast, lunch, and dinner; house cleaning, and so on.

If you allow yourself to be convinced that you **cannot** allow another to do the work for you, then you can **expect** to lose sight of your target fairly easily and regularly. Instead of pushing on toward your goal, you'll switch to making sure you can finish all the menial tasks you refuse to let someone else do.

Learn early the tasks that can be dropped, given to someone else, or **must** be handled by you. This is called appropriate prioritizing and delegation. Outsource the tasks that you don't enjoy doing to others who could do them better and faster than you can. The moment you learn to let some of your responsibilities go to others is the moment you'll find yourself moving faster in the direction you want to go.

Visit www.paradeethomas.com for more resources to discover your talents.

PRINCIPLE #6

Do Something You've Never Done

It is hard to fail, but it is worse never to have tried to succeed.
—Theodore Roosevelt

If you're reading this book, I can assume that your goal is something you've never achieved. If you've reached an impasse within your career, what you did to get you so far won't be enough to take you further. If it was, you wouldn't have reached the impasse.

This is the part of the book where I start talking in extremes and make cautious people a little uneasy. It's because it's right now that you'll realize that Reinventing Yourself isn't about how many books you've read or how many seminars you've attended.

It's about what you **do**.

Reading memoirs and watching inspiring films will only take you so far. The rest requires **action**. I'm not talking about mental action but **physical** work and decisions.

What you do will plunge you into a place you've never been before. You know that, which is probably why you've never taken a step in the right direction, but chosen to stay on your current path. I've got to tell you something though:

**If you want something you've never had,
you've got to do something you've never done.**

That is the basis for this sixth principle. I'm no longer talking about mental tricks and affirmation that give you a warm and fuzzy feeling. I'm talking about facing your fears, counting the costs, and leaping in head first.

Feel the fears and do it anyway. Let go of old routines, you know, the ones that keep you from reaching your goal, and **make** room for new activities that are aligned with your goals and new focus.

I can picture readers glossing over these lines. If this isn't the first book you've read about success and facing your fears, chances are you read the words in past books with the same passivity that you have right now.

Some people like to read more than one book—and that's fine. It's helpful to see multiple different views on the same topic. At some point though, you'll have to acknowledge procrastination for what it really is.

Letting go of what you know is hard, and it's scary. It's okay to admit this. What we can't see or predict is daunting to even the best of us. The difference is that those who make it, face that fear and all the what-ifs.

Truth be told, if you're tuned to the right station, all those what-ifs will barely register. Your RAS simply won't pick it up; you'll be too focused on receiving input that is related to your top priority: Reinvent Yourself.

When we cling to the old way and stale sameness, we don't grow. We remain the same—discontent and stuck in the same routine, running in the same old rut. You can only break this habit by making room for new things to come into your life.

Have you ever been in a stuffy room? The air is old, musty, and gross. You don't freshen the place by placing a fan in the room to blow around the same old funk, do you? Absolutely not! You open a window or door to let in **new** air.

I said earlier that our minds were our only limit. That wasn't a little catch phrase I meditated on for hours so that you could print it out and stick it to a refrigerator as a little reminder. It is truth!

Even money can be used as an excuse to limit people's successes. Out of fear we can create artificial boundaries and limitations in our lives. The worst part is that we actually believe them.

Just like the old saying goes: **Where there's a will, there's a way.**

Contact mentors and people who have travelled this road before you. Be open to ideas that you never saw before. Train your brain to seek out this "new-ness" by making it your priority. It'll single out elements that are relevant to your target.

Did you know that a torpedo needs to be **moving** in order to access the guidance system within it? While stationary, the guidance system won't work.

Think of your navigation system as running on the same type of platform. It's not enough to think. Yes, counting costs and planning is good—at first. After that, you've simply got to roll up your sleeves, and get to work.

Everything takes work.

This is probably one of the most disappointing truths in this book. Don't be afraid to make mistakes. Imperfect results are perfectly acceptable. They're proof that you are taking action. Don't even be afraid of failure. It helps your next try be even more successful. Just keep taking action and keep adjusting the steps along the way.

For more resources, visit www.paradeethomas.com

PRINCIPLE #7
Never Give Up

Success is not final, failure is not fatal: it is the courage to continue that counts.
—Winston Churchill

This seventh principle can easily be mistaken for some empty motivational saying. It seems that most famous quotes involve some degree of looking at obstacles as life's smaller puzzles and conquests, and the real challenge is simply staying focused and never giving up.

These are more than just feel-good words. It's a universal principle that **will** deliver if you are patient **and** diligent. You will find no greater challenge in your life to persevere **against** the grain when you are trying to cut a new trail.

To give up is to cut the momentum circuit! Set back and unexpected mishaps are inevitable. These are part of growth. You need to keep moving because you can't steer a parked car. No course correction can happen if you stand still.

> "A step in the wrong direction is better
> than staying on the spot all our life.
> Once you are moving forward you
> can correct your course as you go.
> Your automatic guidance system cannot
> guide you when you stand still."
>
> Maxwell Maltz

Just think about it. You're stepping into new and uncharted territory. Sure, someone has probably already been there before, but it's easier to convince yourself that others were more capable and more qualified than you.

It makes sense to tell yourself that they had the tools. I'm sure you've heard this phrase before: the grass is always greener on the other side. The truth of the matter is: the grass is greener where you water it.

One of life secrets is to make the most of what we have in front of us. There is no one fixed way of how to "do" life. You can 'do" it any way you want. If you achieve the things you want and the things you desire—if you can say that you are truly happy and not constantly searching for something else— then you've found it. You figured it out!

These are the successes we see around us. They inspire us, motivate us, and encourage us to pursue our deepest unspoken dreams so that we can be happy. But the next day when we wake up, where is our resolve?

Is it still back on our pillows, waiting for us to pick up and dream about later? Or is it something we remind ourselves of daily, hourly, or even minute-by-minutes to keep on track?

I understand that many people face extreme hardships throughout their lives. Unwanted pregnancies, job losses, death, and illnesses of close friends or family members. These are things that are simply unavoidable in some cases, tragic in others, but all are a natural process in life.

Don't wish that your burden in life were lighter or easier. Instead wish that your back was stronger. But don't stop there; **make** your back stronger through diligence, perseverance, and employing these seven principles that are sure to guide you to personal success.

For more resources, visit www.paradeethomas.com

FINAL NOTE

It had long since come to my attention that people of accomplishment rarely sat back and let things happen to them. They went out and happened to things.

—Leonardo da Vinci

We've just covered seven principles to reinvent your life. Finishing this book is one thing, but actually seeing your goal to fruition is another.

The goal in life isn't to read as many books or view as many educational videos as possible. It's to be the you that makes you most happy and most complete. Reading principles that you've never heard before is one thing. Putting them into practice is another.

I leave you with a simple challenge. Well, perhaps it's not that simple after all.

**I challenge you to challenge yourself.
Say YES to your dream.**

Face your fears and all your doubts, worries, and insecurities about your future and rewrite it today, starting right now.

Choose a destination, be bold and do not give yourself a limit. If money and time, the two biggest restrictions, were no longer issues, what would you be pursuing? Whatever your answer, you've just discovered your passion. Is it worth reinventing your life for?

I've been fortunate to have worked in an occupation I love for a long time. It has allowed me to see a wide variety of people and learn about a lot of different experiences and challenges that many people have faced in their adult lives.

I can tell you that nothing has burdened me more than to see people biting their lips and white-knuckling life until they reach an age where they can relax. Do you know the type I'm describing?

They look forward to some elusive day in their futures for their lives to finally come together and "make sense." By the time they reach this foggy place in their lives, they're too embittered and jaded to appreciate or care about it.

This is no way to live. Stop letting life happen to you. The greatest, best-kept secret is that life is what **you** make of it.

Separate yourself from the people who keep you thinking that this is the best it's going to get, that you'll never be more than what you are right now. Get the most out of each day— don't ever waste even one! What are you waiting for? Get up—go!

For more resources, visit www.paradeethomas.com

MY WISH FOR YOU

Wherever you are in life, you know that *who* you are and *where* you are is not enough. You want to go further, to take one more step, to turn another corner. You've tried many times to break free, to become someone you want to be and walk a different path. What is it that's keeping you back? Maybe you've tasted the sweet flavour of success, only to have it ripped from you as you hit a wall, unable to push through or go around. How can you make it to the other side or leap onto a higher plane?

I sincerely hope that you will give it one more try! Apply the basic principles in this book to re-invent yourself, your business or your career. I have used these principles re-inventing my clients' business and my personal life many times over. They will work for you too.

I would love to read your success story someday.

Paradee Thomas

Books in this Series

Re-Invent Yourself

Business, Career and Personal Transformation

Book One
7 Transforming Principles to Increase Happiness, Work–Life Balance and the Self–Worth of Your Inner Child

Book Two
7 Steps to Self Transformation with Ease and Grace Reconnect with Your True Super Power

Book Three
The Secrets of Self Motivation Keep on Keeping on to Create a Life you Love; a Career you Excel in; a Rewarding Business

For more resources, visit www.paradeethomas.com

ABOUT THE AUTHOR

Paradee Thomas is an International #1 Best Selling author, speaker and coach. This book – Re-Invent Yourself: Business, Career and Personal Transformation has reached #1 Best Selling status in 29 categories and across 5 countries in US, UK, Australia, Canada and Germany.

For a period of over 25 years, Paradee Thomas consulted to large corporate clients on IT Projects and Business Management. Specialisation in transformation is her hallmark. Paradee was often given a difficult job of turning around a project or business operation with hundreds of people involved.

Paradee has instilled the key elements of transformational success principles that she has learned and implemented in her clients' Business over the past 25 years and applied them to her personal life over and over again. The principles outlined in this book will save you years of trial and error! You can benefit from the content of this book without having to spend years of your life experimenting.

Why do we have to Re-invent ourselves, you may ask! We all have to evolve with time to increase happiness, personal fulfilment and self-worth. Change does not have to be hard. The Principles in this book will help you transform your business, career and personal life with ease and fun. Transformation is a journey and it can be so rewarding when you know how.

Made in the USA
Columbia, SC
02 October 2023